Hanford Abram Edson

The Church

God's Building

Hanford Abram Edson

The Church
God's Building

ISBN/EAN: 9783337294472

Printed in Europe, USA, Canada, Australia, Japan

Cover: Foto ©Lupo / pixelio.de

More available books at **www.hansebooks.com**

The Church God's Building.

A HISTORICAL DISCOURSE,

DELIVERED, DECEMBER 22, 1867,

AT THE OPENING OF THE NEW CHAPEL

OF THE

SECOND PRESBYTERIAN CHURCH,

INDIANPOLIS, INDIANA,

By HANFORD A. EDSON,

PASTOR OF THE CHURCH,

———— • • • ————

INDIANAPOLIS:
DOUGLASS & CONNER, JOURNAL OFFICE PRINTERS.

1868.

EDSON, HANFORD ABRAM, 1837-
The church God's building. A historical
discourse, delivered, December 22, 1867, at the
opening of the new chapel of the Second Presbyterian church, Indianpolis[!], Indiana.   Indianapolis,Douglass,1868.
18p.

4/6

The Church God's Building.

A HISTORICAL DISCOURSE,

DELIVERED, DECEMBER 22, 1867,

AT THE OPENING OF THE NEW CHAPEL

OF THE

SECOND PRESBYTERIAN CHURCH,

INDIANPOLIS, INDIANA,

BY HANFORD A. EDSON,

PASTOR OF THE CHURCH,

• ◦ •

INDIANAPOLIS:
DOUGLASS & CONNER, JOURNAL OFFICE PRINTERS.
1868.

DISCOURSE.

1. *Corinthians* 3:9. " Ye are God's building."

The Apostle wished the Corinthian Christians gratefully to remember God as the maker of all their strength. " Paul is nothing," he says. " Apollos is nothing. Man is nothing. The true leader and helper is God. Your redemption is from Him. By Him you were called into the kingdom of His Son. He adopted you as His children. He establishes you in the faith. What you are you are by Him. He has builded you up."

This thought, so impressively urged upon the disciples at Corinth by their faithful friend and teacher, is the one to which our minds are carried, and to which they are held, on this happy day. This church is God's building. Its beginning, its growth, its usefulness, its present strength, are all of Him. To God let our hearts now and ever ascribe the praise.

We shall be the more disposed to rejoice in God as our Builder if we make ourselves minutely acquainted with our history. At least a cursory review of the past is suggested, if it be not demanded, by the present occasion. To-day, with much hopefulness, we enter upon a new era. From the point to which we have now at last been brought, our path seems to widen. It is natural to pause and look back over the road we have travelled. We might find, too, an additional reason for gathering up the story of the past to-day, in the fact that those who alone remember it cannot long be here. It might soon be impossible to learn with any fullness or accuracy what our history has been. We will devote the hour, then, to a historical survey, and

4

it will be seen, with every glance we take, how true it is that this church is " God's building."

Indianapolis, within the memory of men still young, was a wilderness of mud and the favorite haunt of ague. In the fall of 1821, when the whole population was prostrated by malarial fevers, the little settlement had acquired a reputation which it did not easily lose—which, indeed, it did its best to maintain for many years. Physicians sought the place eagerly and found enough to do. The unusual energy and courage of the inhabitants were severely tried by the manifest unwholesomeness of the climate. Many came only to shiver and shudder and hurry away. In 1838 mud and ague were still predominant. One could discover but little promise then of any great prosperity. There was a population of only twenty-five hundred. Uncommon mental activity was shown, and there was a delightful social life; but everything pleasant and good had to struggle hard for existence. The village had no gas, no railroad, no daily newspaper. It could hardly be said to have a book-store, or a pavement, or a daily mail. It seemed difficult to tell why human beings should persist in living here in the woods, almost shut away from communication with the world. But just at this point it is that our history begins.

The rise of Presbyterianism here is nearly co-eval with the origin of the town itself. The lots now covered by the city were laid out in the spring of 1821, and first offered for sale in October of that year. The first formal Presbyterian organization was established less than two years later, July 5, 1823. Fifteen years later still our own society was formed.

The Second Presbyterian Church, Indianapolis, was organized by Rev. James H. Johnson, Nov. 19, 1838, in the Marion County Seminary, a small brick building standing, until 1860, at the south-west corner of University Square. The division of the Presbyterian Church in the United States, occurring at Philadelphia in May of the

same year, was the event out of which this organization grew. Those persons connected with the original Presbyterian society here, who sympathized with the Constitutional Assembly, thought it necessary to establish a separate society in harmony with that body. After many conferences and much reflection, the church was accordingly founded on the d iy mentioned. The original members of the church were but fifteen in number. Their names are as follows: Bethuel F. Morris, Daniel Yandes, Luke Munsell, Lawrence M. Vance, Mary J. Vance, Sidney Bates, William Eckert, Alexander H. Davidson, Robert Mitchell, William S. Hubbard, Joseph F. Holt, Margaret R. Holt, John L. Ketcham, Jane Ketcham, and Catharine Merrill. Of these, only two are now in the society, viz : Daniel Yandes and William S. Hubbard.

It was with much difficulty that the little band, thus united in the faith of the gospel, secured a leader. On the 20th of November, the day after the organization, they issued a call to Rev. Sylvester Holmes, of New Bedford, Mass. The call was declined. Some weeks later, Jan. 15, 1839, they invited Rev. John C. Young, of Danville, Ky., to become their pastor. But this overture was also un-successful. On the 13th of May, of the same year, they called to the pastorate Rev. Henry Ward Beecher, then of Lawrenceburg, Indiana. This call was accepted, and the first pastor entered upon his work here July 31, 1839.

The society though small, was vigorous and hopeful. The few who composed it were ready to stand bravely about the man who had come to serve them in the Master's name. They now numbered thirty-two, having received, since the organization, seventeen additional members. With these the labor began. The County Seminary was occupied from the first as the place of worship. It was there that the pastor's first sermon was heard, and there, for a twelve-month, the church remained. They then went into their own edifice, the present High-school building, north-west corner of Circle and Market streets, occupy-

ing for a time the lecture-room. Soon, however, the house was completed, and the dedication occurred October 4, 1840. The church was now, as it seemed, securely established. The small room in the Seminary had become too strait for them, and with their increased facilities for work, in the new building, they looked forward with most cheerful anticipations. Nor were they disappointed. There had already been a pleasant activity and growth. Steadily accessions had come from other churches, and some had been gathered from the world. This constant, though not remarkable, progress continued through the year 1841. As the new year opened signs of peculiar promise appeared, and in the early spring of 1842 a revival began, more noticeable, perhaps, than any that this church or this community has seen. The whole town was pervaded by the influences of religion. For many weeks the work continued with unabated power, and at three communion seasons, held successively in February, March and April, 1842, nearly one hundred persons were added to the church on profession of their faith. This was God's work. It is not improper, however, to speak of the pastor in that revival, as he is remembered by some of the congregation— plunging through the wet streets; his trowsers stuffed in his muddy boot-legs; earnest, untiring, swift; with a merry heart, a glowing face, and a helpful word for every one; the whole day preaching Christ to the people where he could find them, and at night preaching still where the people were sure to find him. It is true that in this revival some wood and hay and stubble were gathered, with the gold and silver and precious stones. As in all new communities, there was special danger of unhealthy excitement. But in general, the results were most happy for the church and for the town. Some of those who have been pillars since found the Saviour in that memorable time. Nor was the awakening succeeded by an immediate relapse. Early in the following year, at the March and April communions, the church had large accessions, as it had also in

1845. There was, indeed, a wholesome and nearly continuous growth up to the time when the first pastor resigned, to accept a call to the Plymouth Congregational Church, in Brooklyn, New York. This occurred August 24, 1847, and on the 19th of the following month Mr. Beecher's labors for the congregation ceased.

The pastorate, thus terminated, had extended through more than eight years. During this time much had been accomplished. The society had built a pleasant house of worship. The membership had advanced from thirty-two to two hundred and seventy-five. What was considered a doubtful enterprise, inaugurated as it had been amidst many prophecies of failure, had risen to an enviable position, not only in the capital, but in the State. The attachment between pastor and people had become peculiarly strong. Mutual toils and sufferings and successes had bound them fast together. Only the demands of a wider field, making duty plain, divided them, and a recent letter proves that the pastor's early charge still keeps its hold upon his heart. It is not to be wondered at that the few of his flock who yet remain among us, always speak of " Henry" with beaming eyes and mellow voice.

The flock was now without a shepherd. From September, 1847, to April, 1848, the pulpit was temporarily supplied by Rev. Shubael Granby Spees. An invitation was then extended to Rev. Clement E. Babb, at the time a student in Lane Seminary, now the very successful editor of the *Christian Herald* at Cincinnati, to preach for the society during the approaching vacation. He came to Indianapolis and commenced work, May 7, 1848. On the 17th of July following he was called to the pastorate, and on the 18th of September, of the same year, was ordained and installed, Rev. Harvey Curtis, preaching the sermon.

The second period of the church's history began during the railroad excitement, which, springing up in 1847 with the completion of the Madison road, did not cease until eight different lines had been put in successful operation.

With this excitement the town grew rapidly. Yet for some time the church made no advancement. Its numbers steadily decreased. The greatly stimulated greed for gain was the bane of spiritual life. In 1850, however, God again visited His people, and there was a considerable increase of strength. During the first half of the next year the progress was still more apparent, so that the society now had nearly reached again the strength reported at the close of the first pastor's administration. The place of worship was full. For further growth there was scarcely room. Steps must be taken, as it seemed, either to make the house larger or to diminish the congregation by sending out a colony. The latter course was advised by the pastor, and at last harmoniously determined upon. After a full interchange of opinion, September 30, 1851 the session resolved that it was desirable and practicable to form a colony and establish here another church of our order. At the same time a line was drawn, "beginning at the northern limits of the city, in the center of Pennsylvania street, thence extending south to the center of Washington street, thence west to the center of Meridian, and thence south to the city limits," and "all members of the church east of said line, together with a portion of the young men resident west thereof" were advised to unite with the colony. The church at once proceeded to act in the matter, and while it was found impossible to effect a geographical division of the congregation, many of the members given to the colony by the resolution of session hesitating to leave the old society, the new enterprise was, notwithstanding, put upon a secure foundation. On the 30th of November, 1851, the following persons, twenty-four in all, were dismissed from the church to form the colony, viz: Samuel Merrill, Catharine Merrill, Julia D. Merrill, Alexander Graydon, Jane C. Graydon, Jennie McKinney Graydon, Mary Ellen Sharpe, John Kelshaw, Elizabeth Kelshaw, Ann Bruce, Robert Mitchell, Barbara Mitchell, Harriet Mitchell, Barbara A. Wiseman, William

Bradshaw, Martha Bradshaw, Robert Stewart, Nancy A.
Stewart, Edward Sinker, Sarah Sinker, W. W. Roberts,
A. W. Roberts, Walter J. Williams, and Isaac F. Wood.
The Fourth Presbyterian Church was accordingly established, on the day just named. Now, after these sixteen
years, the child has attained a position and a character in
which the parent may well rejoice. It has made its way,
through difficulties and conflicts, which at times made
many fear that the formation of another society was too
early undertaken. But now it is clear that it was God's
design thus to build us up.

Though weakened by its contributions to the colony
the church was still vigorous and hopeful. It was severely
tried, however, by the failure of the pastor's health, which
required him to be absent from his pulpit for several weeks
in the spring of 1852, and which finally compelled him to
give up his charge. His resignation, which once before
had been refused, was again presented, December 26, 1852,
and on the first of January following, his labors for the
congregation, which had continued nearly five years, were
closed.

It was exceedingly desirable that a successor should be
secured without delay. The pulpit remained vacant, however, for a full year. During this period it was occa-
sionally supplied by the former pastor, and by various
other clergymen. Not until the autumn were steps taken
to secure a settled minister. A call was sent, October 20,
to Rev. Thornton A. Mills, which was accepted, and he
entered upon the pastorate, January 1, 1854. On the 19th
of the succeeding month he was installed, Rev. Philip S.
Cleland preaching the sermon. Meanwhile the strength
of the church had been much depleted. To the Assembly of 1854 but one hundred and sixteen members were
reported, less than half the previous working force. This
was really a startling decline. The dependence of the
people of God upon the stated means of grace, and the
weakness of a church without a leader had been abund-

antly proven. With the coming of the new pastor the skies grew brighter, however, and to the Assembly of 1855, one hundred and thirty-one members were reported, a gain of seventeen during the year. This rate of progress continued. There were no unusual displays of God's power; but there was a steady increase in numbers, and christians evidently grew upon the " strong meat," not for " babes," with which they were constantly fed. Towards the close of 1856, however, Dr. Mills was elected Secretary of the General Assembly's Committee on Education, and was constrained to present to the church his resignation. The society, in reluctantly accepting it, adopted a minute express-ing their sense of the faithfulness and ability which had characterized his labors here. On the 9th of February, 1857, Presbytery dissolved the relation between pastor and peo-ple, and soon after Dr. Mills took up his Secretary's pen in the city of New York.

Of those who have been bishops over you, Thornton A. Mills is the only one not now living. He fell dead, from a stroke of apoplexy, June 19, 1867, as he was stepping from the ferry-boat at Hoboken, New Jersey. He had an honest, solid, vigorous intellect; a trustworthy, and even prophetic, judgment; a will that would break before it bent. That his heart was generous, sufficiently appeared in the fact that, though born in a southern State, his opposition to every form of human slavery was always remarkably earnest and uncompromising. With few graces of person or of manner, his superiority was undoubted. As a preacher he was plain, but unusually strong. Sometimes he was elo-quent. You who heard him remember distinctly yet many of his sermons. His discourse on Church Extension, before the General Assembly, put a new mind into our whole church. The present ef-ion and valorous spirit of our Presbyterian ly sprung from his brain. The country, he west, owes him a heavy debt of grati-

Upon Dr. Mills' removal, the Church, warned by the experience of the recent vacant year, soon sought a minister. August 6, 1857 it gave a call to Rev. George P. Tindall, who had supplied the pulpit since the first of the previous month. The call was at once accepted, though the installation was delayed until June 9, 1859, upon which occasion Rev. Edward Scofield preached the sermon. For a time there was nothing specially to be noticed in the affairs of the Church. Early in 1858, however, the seed of the word began rapidly to grow. That was a year of revival throughout the land, and it was one of the most prosperous years of our history. From April 1858, to April 1859, there were fifty-three accessions on profession of faith, besides sixteen by letter, and the membership rose from one hundred and forty-six to two hundred and two. Nor was there growth in numbers merely. The gain in spiritual life and power, by which every work must be tried, was remarkable. Though in the succeeding twelvemonth there was an evident decrease of activity, the influence of the awakening was still visible. Indeed we may even yet trace the marks it made upon the characters of many who are here.

But you will remember that this was a period of national excitements and alarms. A hot presidential contest in the fall of 1860, was followed in April of the next year, by the breaking out of the rebellion. The war seemed to swallow up everything. Here upon the border, where the perils were greatest, the excitements too were most intense. It was at least natural that the church should suffer in the general confusion. From your pulpit, however, then as afterwards, you always heard the earnest tones of christian patriotism, and you lost but little, even in numbers. Some of your best young men you gave to the army and navy; among whom it is right that I should mention here, Lieutenant Colonel George W. Meikel, who was killed upon the picket line in front of Richmond, and Lieutenant Thomas V. Webb, who died in the service.

In the midst of this troublous time it was that the

Church lost its pastor. His work here, commenced more than six years before, ended September 27, 1863, and he immediately removed to take charge of an important Church at Ypsilanti, Michigan, which he still retains.

We have now reached a period concerning which the records are more full. The present pastor was called November 5, 1863, and began his ministry among you January 17, 1864. He was installed April 26, 1865. When this pastorate began society was still distracted by the war, and there were many things to discourage a worldly judgment. There was, however, more than ordinary attention to the gospel, and all the services of the Church increased in interest. This progress continued through February and March, when it became necessary to make additional appointments for preaching and for prayer. Many of you will long remember the delightful quietness and fervor of those gatherings where God was pleased to show us the power of His son in saving sinners. Immediately following them, at the communion in April, and at the subsequent one in July, more than twenty were added to the Church from the world. Most of these were young men and women.

The strength derived from these tokens of God's favor was permanent. It gave us new hope. When the next year opened not a few were pleading before the mercy-seat that God would revive us again. At first no answer came to our petitions. We heard how the deaf and dumb were in other places seeking the physician. We heard how now as aforetime He spake the word only and they were healed. Yet the deaf ears to which we spoke were not unstopped, and no scales seemed to be falling from any eyes. Early in February, however, almost without warning, indeed without any warning but that which comes to one who is most in sympathy with Christ's spirit, and can most clearly discern spiritual things, the truth seemed suddenly to gain new power, and the Lord's miracles of heal-

ing were wrought among us again. Some here to-day look back to those early months of 1865 as they look back to no other time, for it was then that they were reconciled to God. At the communion in April eighteen persons made choice of Christ publicly and came into our fellowship.

This again renewed our faith. It was another pledge that though it is with God's spirit as with the wind, which "bloweth where it listeth," it is certain too that He will not permit His word to fail. During the rest of the year, as through the previous twelvemonth, there was a steady growth, indicating, to those who cared to watch, a real and healthful vitality. The autumn of 1865, and the first months of 1866, were signalized, as you have not forgotten, by general and powerful revivals throughout the country. Our own community had part in the blessing. God was in this Church once more. Often the air seemed oppressive, so was it penetrated and loaded with the Divine influence. I can now recall two or three evenings especially, when the Almighty Lord seemed almost visibly to work through His creatures; when it was only necessary to speak out the gospel plainly, and it quickly took tight hold of men; tore them straight away from their refuges of lies, and carried them over to the sure foundations in Christ. On the last sabbath in March, 1866, the space in front of the old pulpit was filled by those who stood there to make their covenant with God. Thus, for three successive years, it was granted you to see the special displays of His grace.

The present year, though in some respects more fruitful than any other the Church has known, has not yet been marked by any scenes of revival. There was a cloud, bigger than a man's hand, before the spring communion, but the showers we had hoped for did not fall. Our work had been much interrupted by the necessary removal from the lecture room to make way for the public schools, the trustees of which had purchased the building. The audience room above we retained for some months longer, the last religious service in the old house being held on the evening

of July 16, 1867, an occasion which your pastor will not be likely soon to forget.

Along with the spiritual growth of the Church, during the present period, there has been every proof of outward and material prosperity. It is to be remembered with especial gratitude that you have been able to do much to extend the influence of the gospel to others in the community. The "Indianapolis Union Mission Sunday School" is largely indebted to the assistance you rendered, both at its organization, and in the erection of the school house at the corner of Meridian and Union streets, which it now occupies. The "Fifth Presbyterian Church" is your child. Its building, at the corner of Michigan and Blackford streets, dedicated May 15, 1864, was erected and furnished, and a numerous sabbath school was organized and sustained there, chiefly by members of this Church. We wish for the enterprise abundant success in the new hands which now direct it. To the "Olivet Presbyterian Church," corner of Union and McCarty streets, we may refer with yet greater interest. This promising society sprang from the conferences of a few gentlemen of the church, called together on the afternoon of June 17 of the present year. At an adjourned meeting, June 22, a committee was appointed and instructed to buy lots and build a chapel in the south-western quarter of the city. The present site was soon selected, and the building was begun in September. On the 20th of October, just passed, it was set apart by your pastor to the worship of God, and by him, one month later, November 20, the Church was organized with twenty-one members. They already have a minister who is earnestly at work, and it now seems that the best and largest results must flow from their harmonious activity.

It thus appears, both from the interior life and outward labors of the Church, what reason we have for gratitude to Him who is our Builder. We may now gather up some general conclusions from our history.

The total number of different persons connected with the

Church since its organization is eight hundred and twelve; of whom three hundred and eigty-six have been received by letter, and four hundred and twenty on profession of their faith. 1823867

The contributions of the society to benevolent objects have amounted to one hundred thousand dollars. For the usual congregational purposes one hundred and thirty thousand dollars have been raised.

Two persons have entered the ministry from our membership: Rev. George Hills White, well known as a former missionary of the American Board, in Turkey, and Rev. Lycurgus Railsback. A third is now at Crawfordsville in course of preparation for the sacred office.

The first elders of the Church were Daniel Yandes and Bethuel F. Morris, who were elected, November 19, 1838, the day of the organization, and Luke Munsell, chosen on the day following. Their successors have been John J. McFarland, John L. Ketcham, Horace Bassett, Samuel Merrill, Alexander Graydon, Henry S. Kellogg, Robert H. King, Thomas R. Case, William S. Hubbard, Robert Nicol, David V. Culley, William N. Jackson, Samuel F. Smith, Enoch C. Mayhew, Edwin J. Peck, John S. Spann, Francis H. Kingsbury. The seven last mentioned constitute the present board. Something more than the record of their names is due to two of those who have thus served the Church and now have risen to the higher services of heaven.

Bethuel F. Morris, elected to the eldership at the organization of the society, worthily occupied the place until his death, February 8, 1864. His death was the first which occurred in the Church during the present pastorate. Judge Morris was one of the early settlers of the town. He had a cultivated mind and pleasing manners. During the first stages of our history, in the absence of a minister, it often fell to him to read a discourse to the congregation gathered in the County seminary. He was a man of remarkable honor. Though modest almost to a fault, and so sensitive

as to prefer the retirement of his study and his home, he was often called by his fellow-citizens to important public trusts, which were discharged with a fidelity that became proverbial. His memory in the community and in the Church is fragrant still.

Samuel Merrill became an elder of the Church September 3, 1816. He removed here at the close of the year 1821, as the seat of government was being transferred from Corydon to this place. He was then Treasurer of State. The services he rendered in that capacity, and afterwards in every enterprise for the advancement of the town, were invaluable. He was the friend of everything generous and good. Having himself studied at Dartmouth College, New Hampshire, he was among the foremost in promoting the cause of education. Noble in his impulses, strict in his integrity, strong in his will, of liberal tastes, and in his piety thorough and uniform, he made himself honorable as a citizen and an office-bearer in the church. At the time of his death, which occurred August 24, 1855, he was an elder in the Fourth Presbyterian Church, to which he had gone with the first colonists from this society.

The Church had no deacons until December 19, 1841, when Alexander H. Davidson and William S. Hubbard, were chosen. Since that time the following persons have held the office: Albert G. Willard, Jacob J. Wiseman, Lawrence M. Vance, Daniel Carlisle, Jacob S. Walker, James M. Yandes, Howard Mills, Joseph B. Wilson, Ezekiel Boyd, George W. Meikel, Alfred D. Clarke, William C. Smith, Charles P. Wilson, Francis H. Kingsbury, John L. Fish and Edward S. Field. Of these the two last named hold the office now.

The sabbath school, which was organized in August, 1839, has been, especially in recent years, the nursery of the Church. A noticeable feature of it has been the large number of young men and women in its classes. It has also had unusual sympathy and support from the older and

more influential members of the society. Its weekly contributions now amount to more than five hundred dollars per annum. The first superintendent of the school was Samuel Merrill. Of his successors mention may be made of two who are no longer among the living: Henry P. Coburn, a native of Vermont, a graduate of Harvard College, a lawyer, a ripe scholar, a large-hearted man; and Dr. Talbott Bullard, whose ardent temperament, wide intelligence, and ready eloquence, matured as they had been by diligent study and extensive travels, made his more recent death an occasion of profound sorrow to the whole community. Other men have served the school with equal devotedness, and its condition was never perhaps as hopeful as it is at the present time.

You will expect me, in conclusion, to give some account, of the beautiful and enduring house of worship which we occupy to-day. It was the original intention to erect the new building on the old site. Plans were drawn for such a structure. Before the enterprise was fully developed, however, there began to be some discussion as to the propriety of a removal northward. Accordingly three or four gentlemen of the society secured the present site upon their own private responsibility, and on the 3d of December the congregation, by a formal vote, decided to remove to this point. The lots previously purchased were immediately turned over to the trustees at cost, though they were eagerly sought by others for a much larger sum. To the gentlemen who so energetically and generously acted in this matter we are greatly indebted. Every day the wisdom of the change of our location has become more apparent. For this edifice ground was broken in the spring of 1864. Much time was prudently taken, however, to perfect the plans, and the corner-stone was not laid until May 12, 1866. Since that date the work has steadily proceeded. But no wasteful haste has been allowed. Nothing has been slighted. The purpose has been to erect a permanent and truthful structure. God, who is the " Builder," has been with us from

the first. At no time has there been any lack of funds. Thus far, too, no serious accident of any kind has occurred in connection with the work. For the completion of the building it is not doubted that the requisite funds will be as cheerfully furnished as the sum already expended has been. Of this we are the more confident, because what has been so excellently done has also been accomplished with singular economy. Those of you who have had the most experience in such affairs will be surprised to learn that the costs have constantly fallen below the estimates. It need hardly be said that for this, as for the beauty of the design and the thoroughness of the whole work, we owe much to the architect, who, in addition to a wholesome professional pride, has been all the while stimulated by his attachment to the society, of which he is a member. To the building committee also,—especially to its treasurer and superintendent,—the warmest thanks are due.

So, my friends, at last we are here. We stand to-day at the opening of a broader path. The wildeness of mud, the ague-stricken settlement, the straggling village in the woods, has become a populous and beautiful city. The feeble society, almost begging permission to live, has grown into a substantial, compact and vigorous Church, with a history back of it, and before it, as we trust, enlarged usefulness in the service of God and mankind. This is a day for thanksgiving. It is also a day for devout consecrations to Christ. Our opportunities are greater than ever before. We were never so well organized as now. The Captain of the host bids us go forward. We ought to pray for hearts attentive to His voice. May He be with us here to the end. May He make the glory of this new temple bright. May the comforts He gave His people in the former sanctuary be here increased. May the grace that there conquered sinners, here with new power prevail. And so to the latest generation may the honor of Him who hath builded us fill the place.